I Help Out My Parents

AMY CULLIFORD

A Crabtree Roots Book

School-to-Home Support for Caregivers and Teachers

This book helps children grow by letting them practice reading. Here are a few guiding questions to help the reader with building his or her comprehension skills. Possible answers appear here in red.

Before Reading:

- What do I think this book is about?
  - I think this book is about helping parents at home.
  - I think this book is about how important it is to do chores at home.
- What do I want to learn about this topic?
  - I want to learn what jobs I can do to help my parents.
  - I want to learn how to help prepare meals at home.

During Reading:

- I wonder why...
  - I wonder why there is so much laundry to wash every week.
  - I wonder why parents have so many jobs to do at home.
- What have I learned so far?
  - I have learned that it's fun to help make dinner.
  - I have learned that gardening is something I can do to help out my parents.

After Reading:

- What details did I learn about this topic?
  - I have learned that I can help clean up when there is a mess.
  - I have learned that it is fun to help out my parents at home.
- Read the book again and look for the vocabulary words.
  - I see the word **parents** on page 3 and the word **dinner** on page 8. The other vocabulary words are found on page 14.

I want to help out my **parents**.

I help with
the **laundry**.

I help out in the **garden**.

I help to make **dinner**.

I help **clean** up.

I like to help out my parents!

Word List
Sight Words

help	make	to
I	my	up
in	out	want
like	the	with

Words to Know

clean

dinner

garden

laundry

parents

34 Words

I want to help out my **parents**.

I help with the **laundry**.

I help out in the **garden**.

I help to make **dinner**.

I help **clean** up.

I like to help out my parents!

I Help Out My Parents

Written by: Amy Culliford
Designed by: Rhea Wallace
Series Development: James Earley
Proofreader: Melissa Boyce
Educational Consultant: Marie Lemke M.Ed.

Photographs:
Shutterstock: TrzyKropy: cover; Pixel-shot: p. 1;VGstockstudio: p.3; TrzyKropy: p. 5; Maria Sbytova: p. 7; wong yu liang: p. 9;Yuri A: p. 11; Odua Images: p. 12

Crabtree Publishing

crabtreebooks.com   800-387-7650
Copyright © 2025 Crabtree Publishing
All rights reserved. No part of this publication may be reproduced, stored in a retrieval system or be transmitted in any form or by any means, electronic, mechanical, photocopying, recording, or otherwise, without the prior written permission of Crabtree Publishing. In Canada: We acknowledge the financial support of the Government of Canada through the Canada Book Fund for our publishing activities.

Printed in the USA
062024/CG20240201

Published in Canada
Crabtree Publishing
616 Welland Ave.
St. Catharines, Ontario
L2M 5V6

Published in the United States
Crabtree Publishing
347 Fifth Ave
Suite 1402-145
New York, NY 10016

Library and Archives Canada Cataloguing in Publication
Available at Library and Archives Canada

Library of Congress Cataloging-in-Publication Data
Available at the Library of Congress

Hardcover: 978-1-0398-3831-4
Paperback: 978-1-0398-3916-8
Ebook (pdf): 978-1-0398-4000-3
Epub: 978-1-0398-4072-0